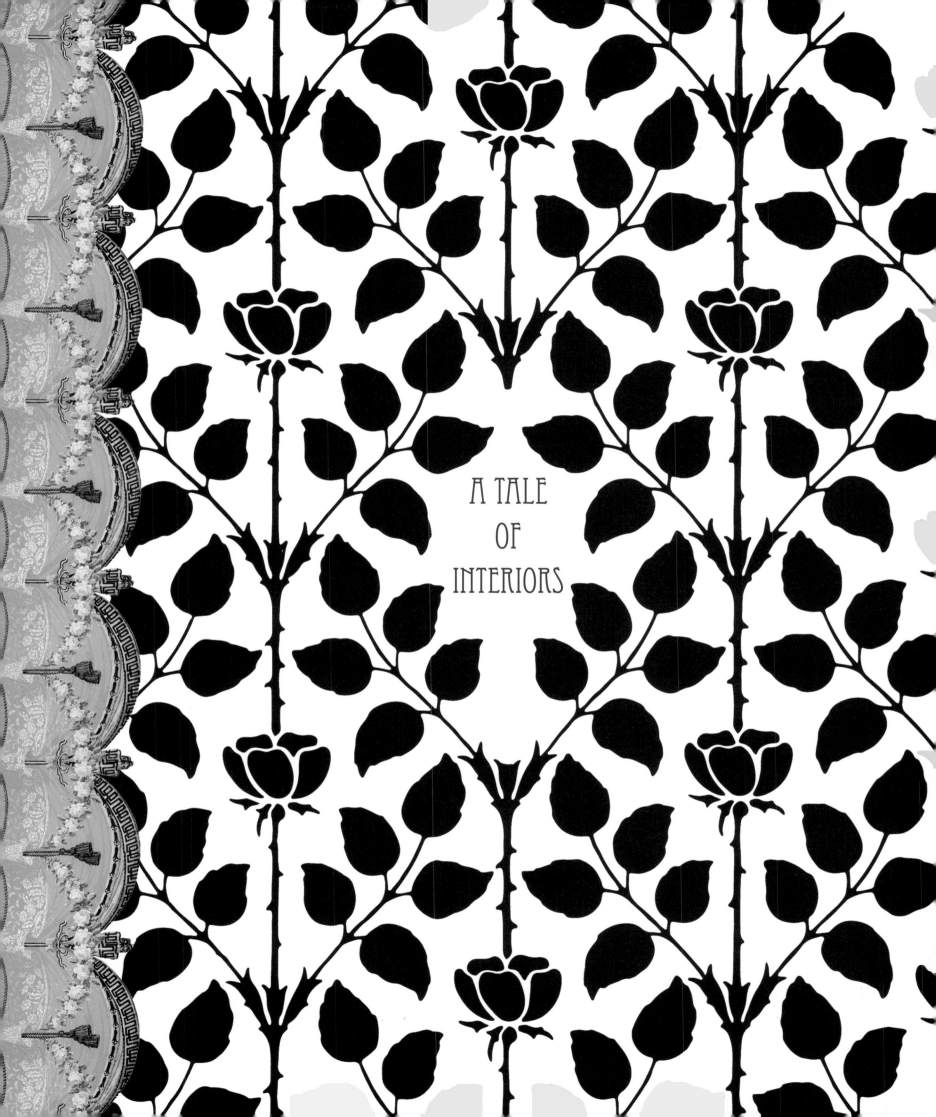

A TALE
OF
INTERIORS

THE ART OF MORE

A TALE

OF 🐍 🐍

INTERIORS

PIERCE & WARD

TEXT BY CATHERINE PIERCE

RIZZOLI
NEW YORK

New York Paris London Milan

FOR
OUR
MOTHERS

A TALE OF INTERIORS

There's much talk of minimalism in design these days: refining, getting rid of, purging . . . reducing and shaving away to the very bare bones of necessity. If one were to compare it to nature—art imitating life—the minimalist movement would be the wide open plain, the empty field covered with snow. Stark, beautiful, and quiet . . . bordering on impersonal. Perhaps it evokes peace for some? Perhaps it invites possibility? But what about those of us who love the forest? The fruition? Possibility bursting forth? Those of us who love a garden in full bloom? The magic in collages

of color, kaleidoscopic patterns, layering of artifacts, and hidden gems? What about the collector? The treasure hunter? The builders of estates and empires? The curators of heirlooms? Surely they are not minimalists!

There is great joy to be found in the find. There is great passion in the hunt. There is beauty in the unfolding of a room that takes the eye dancing from one piece to the next, swirling over velvets of peach and gold, skittering along striped walls, gliding over glass and marble, and finally dipping and tumbling onto floors flocked with Persian rugs made skillfully soft with tradition and love.

So while some obsess over paring down, whittling away, and emptying out, you'll find us filling up, piling high, and stocking troves. This book will teach you about organized abundance, ungaudy decadence, unbridled collections—and just a dash of restraint for good measure. Pierce & Ward will teach you . . . the Art of More.

CHAPTER ONE

IN THE BEGINNING

olor can evoke emotion. Detail can conjure memory.

Soft peaches and olive-y greens remind Louisa Pierce of her Alabama childhood, racing across the sprinkler-soaked lawns of her great aunt's home. When the mosquitoes drove them inside, she and her sisters would fly down amber-lit hallways, collapsing onto green silk–swathed sofas stuffed fat with down. Though her own parents' means were meager, it was a priority of Louisa's mother, Anne, to have a beautiful home. Rooms were regularly rearranged and repainted. Furniture refinished and repurposed. Could the living room and dining room swap places? Won't know until we try! Being an artist, Anne recognized the power of placement and color. This gift was passed on to Louisa along with the art of the bargain shop. Yard sales were regularly scoured for antiques and art. Thrift stores provided vintage Chinese vases that were made into lamps and sets of dining chairs that only needed a glossy coat of paint to be special again. An embroidered shawl draped over an old table could warm up a room in an instant. Necessity was the mother of invention

and of reinvention for Louisa and she learned that you could do a lot with a little if you developed a keen eye for color and beautiful pieces.

Soft grays and creams remind Emily Ward of her youth. Barefoot, sun-bleached walks along bone-colored sands. Kneeling and squinting to find smooth stones and shells in bright, foamy tides. Her favorite feeling was fresh, clean cotton wrapped around salty shoulders after a day at the beach. She remembers the soft clattering of her mother's bangles as she arranged lilies that would grace the center of their long dining table that her dad nicknamed "Pass the Gravy." The air was always perfumed with newly cut flowers as Joni Mitchell sang them through the afternoon. A few times a year her family would take trips across the border into Mexico and come home with handmade clay pots and intricately stitched blankets and pillows. Emily's early days in design leaned heavily on layered, creamy whites until Louisa encouraged her to embrace color. Now, every shade of ocean from her California childhood is reflected in her current palette: translucent green, murky navy, and turbulent gray along with the soft burning pinks, oranges, and golds of the sun setting over water.

Pierce & Ward consistently draw from their own past for inspiration, which reflects lovingly in their work. History can be woven into patterns and palettes, memories cracked open through touch, texture, and feel. Pierce & Ward seek to re-create the early awakening of the senses by bringing things into the home that remind everyone of the wonderful perfection of nature and the thrill of new experience.

CHAPTER TWO

TWIN FLAMES

ierce & Ward came to be in the manner that generally occurs when people get out of the universe's way. Two young ladies with zero aspirations to be business-women and a strong inclination toward New York City nightlife adventures met in the whiskey glow of the infamous basement of the now-defunct Manhat-tan establishment called The Cabin. Alarm bells went off in the primal part of their boozy brains when their eyes absorbed each other's familial features, triggering tribal attraction and sisterlike synergy. It was a double vision on the rocks, a swift bosom-buddy blossom-ing, a determined destiny knocking on a speakeasy door. Emily, meet Louisa. Louisa, meet Emily. Little did they know that soon their last names would be connected with an elegant ampersand and on the lips of superstars and supermodels, printed on crisp card stock and in glossy magazines, and stitched onto fringed down pillows of their own design.

Sometimes the shabbiest, dankest dives are the birthplaces of brilliance. Sometimes two towheads are much better than one. Sometimes the things that one may lack are absent on purpose so another may fill them with puzzle-lock precision, thus creating a team of dreams. Let this story serve as a reminder that coincidence and fate ride a razor-sharp edge and that by leaning in the right direction, it's possible to slip sweetly down the rabbit hole of a charmed life.

New York City served them well but, over time, Louisa and Emily found themselves longing for larger living spaces. Five-hundred-square-foot apartments offered them little room to stretch their creative legs. After exhausting each corner, rearranging, repainting, and redoing for the trillionth time, they realized that in order to expand they must pack up and fly south. Where could they go that would afford them homes with foyers and lounges? Closets they could twirl in, tubs they could sink in, and stairwells that would lead them to bedrooms and attics? Porches and decks for warm summer nights? Yards for gardens and stargazing and catching fireflies? All the things they had sacrificed to live in the Big Apple. Their priorities were steadily shifting from wild nights on concrete streets to the comforts of an intentional life, one they could build cozily around themselves and place their hearts proudly on the mantel. They were growing up and settling down with style and grace. They needed a town that would nurture their aspirations and flourish along with them. A place that was affordable but still rich with inspiration. They settled on a city that was growing fast and would set the pace of their career trajectory. A place as eclectic as their taste. A place where rock stars and Republicans shopped for vegetables in the same aisle. A little bit country, a little bit rock and roll. A little bit shabby and increasingly chic . . . Nashville.

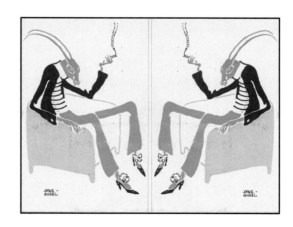

BEST-LAID PLANS

EMILY WARD

No matter how much preplanning we do, we never end up exactly where we thought we would. Rooms start to take on a life of their own and each new piece that is brought in can influence a decision. It's important to have mood boards and a vision to guide you, but it's just as important to remain open to shifts.

MAKE IT PERSONAL

◆ Including keepsakes and personal items in your design will help you feel connected to the rooms. It's a great way to make yourself feel instantly at home and it invites your guests to get to know you better.

◆ Dig out family photos and drawings and mat and frame the special ones. Feature them in gallery walls along with eclectic art.

◆ Line the upper shelves of the kitchen with inherited china. Patterned plates look quite striking hung in rows along the wall.

◆ Go to your local bookstore and find beautiful books on art, architecture, and photography to display on your coffee table. Choose ones that have meaning for you. This is another invitation for your guests to explore what moves you.

◆ Heirloom furniture is wonderful when mixed with newer pieces. It is a nod to where you came from and it's infused with a warmth and energy that is sometimes lacking in modern furniture.

GOOD VIBRATIONS

LOUISA PIERCE

You have to get things into a room and see how their energies play off each other. Something can look great on paper but then fall flat in the home. An open mind and experimental spirit are key when designing a space.

WHERE THE MAGIC HAPPENS

◆ We like to include beautiful old books on almost every shelf we decorate. A set of vintage novels adds richness to every space. Gold-embossed titles and lettering provide a little glamour to what could be a boring display.

◆ Floor-to-ceiling bookshelves give a room height and grandeur. Framing a bed or sofa with built-ins creates instant coziness and access to your favorites reads.

◆ The bigger the bedside table, the better. Double up on lamps . . . one for beauty, one for convenience. Have a tray with everything you need within reach including a little vase of fresh flowers.

◆ We love to add a gorgeous bedspread or tapestry folded at the foot of the bed. It's a perfect opportunity to play with pattern layering. Tie it in with a few fringed, down-filled throw pillows for good measure.

◆ A long bench at the foot of the bed is also a must. It's beautiful and functional. Try a contrasting style from that of the headboard so it doesn't feel like a set. For example, if you choose an upholstered headboard, go for a wooden bench, and vice versa.

 BEHIND THE CURTAIN

LOUISA: I always wanted to be a designer. When I was eight years old I made a design book. My mom would get *House Beautiful*, and all these 1980s design magazines, and I just tore out pictures and made a little design book. I was building my dream home.

EMILY: This explains everything. I don't remember anything from when I was a very little kid. But I loved white. I remember I had a pair of white Keds and I would walk around really carefully so I wouldn't get them dirty. Because we only got a new pair of shoes every six months.

L: It's so funny. The bedroom I chose for my dream house was blue and stark-white toile. It was all matching—the bedding and the curtains. And my home was going to be very formal. Like, fancy-*schmancy*. Fabric everywhere, ruffles, tassels. And everything was stark white, which I hate now. And royal blue. Which I also hate.

E: She's always like [*in bourgeois accent*], "Oh, that's too white. And I only like blue if it's a dusty French blue!"

L: Then my mom threw away my design book at some point [*pretending to cry*]. Like it was a *piece of trash!*

E: I was such a tomboy. I loved black. I was kind of emotional. Still am.

L: You still are.

E: I was less into color and fabric and more into the space. I would constantly move my bed around and reorganize all the furniture. Once a week. By the way, I never thought I'd be a designer. I wanted to be a criminal defense attorney. But I did do all of my friends' rooms in college. It was my specialty. I lived in a beautiful old house with two of my girlfriends on Parker Street, right off College Avenue, in Berkeley.

I paid extra so I could have the room with the really big windows. I had a big bed and my TV was hiding in the armoire and everything was perfect and white. Clean floral pillows. Did my laundry every day. My parents gave us old furniture. The place was really put together so everyone was always over at our house. But I didn't get into design again until I moved to Nashville. That's when I started to get obsessed.

L: The first room I designed was my basement bedroom when I was fourteen. It had ivory plush wall-to-wall carpet and I decked out the bathroom in *W Magazine* tear-outs.

E: Ohhhh, chic.

L: So chic! It was all black-and-white photos, totally collaged, lots of Bridget Hall and Kate Moss. I had a trunk at the end of my bed that was my grandma's. It was beautiful. I didn't even ask my mom, but I painted it in zebra stripes! And I had purple crushed velvet curtains I bought at a cheap fabric store.

E: *Purple?!*

L: And I had the canopy bed that I was actually born in. And my Beatles poster over my turntable. I remember I had to have an arched, swan-neck faucet for my sink. I wanted it so bad. We went to Home Depot and bought it for, like, thirty bucks! I was so excited. My room was fabulous. I had three friends that made me do collage walls for them, too.

E: I remember when I was a kid we rented different houses and moved so many times, but we always had the same furniture. It's the same furniture I have in my house now. My living room couch is from before I was born; my parents found it on the street. My mom was a

major entertainer. We had so many people at our house, every day. It was a great vibe, there was always music blasting throughout the house. She was always cooking something delicious. People came at all hours, poured themselves drinks. We had beautiful handblown glasses from the Czech Republic that my mom sold in her store.

L: What was her store called?

E: Me Gusta.

L: I love that!

E: I named it. It was in Laguna. She ran it. I don't like to talk about it because it stressed her out so much. There wasn't a lot of walking traffic, so making rent was hard. She sold candles and glasses and some frames and furniture. Some old, some new. A little gift/home store. It was for fun, but it stressed her out. She had a problem with clothes shopping. Just a couple weeks before she died, she was in a wheelchair and could barely speak and she bought a $6,000 dress! She said [*in a Scottish accent*], "I want to look good for people coming to say goodbye to me." A week before she died she made my dad buy her red Prada slip-ons. I still have those.

L: You are literally your mother. When you were eight months pregnant with twins, waddling down the streets of New York, your ankles were this big and you were like, "I need to go into that store!" And you were trying on maternity outfits that were the most expensive . . . At eight months! So absurd.

E: I'm so much like my mom.

L: How long have you been obsessed with laundry?

E: [*Cackling*] As long as I can remember! My mom would say, "You're so good at folding!" My whole family calls me Laundry Lil'.

L: I have a bit of a laundry thing. My favorite memory was sitting on the couch, watching *I Love Lucy*, and my mother, Mamaw, would come in with the hot, fresh-out-of-the-dryer clothes, and dump them on me.

E: Ah, the best.

L: But I never folded them! Ha!

E: My dad is the English boarding school type so it was always like [*in an English accent*], "Yup, tidy up, make your bed, do the laundry, do this, do that." He'd come into our rooms in the morning and it would be freezing cold and he'd rip the comforter off. "Get up!" Then you'd have to make the bed perfect. On Saturdays he'd start blasting music so early, put all the dining room chairs on the table, and he'd be mopping the floors. That's where I got it from.

L: So your dad was the clean freak, not your mom?

E: Yeah, my dad was. My mom, she had messy drawers. It all looked pretty on top, but it was like a mess underneath.

L: Like *me*.

E: *Mm-hmm!*

L: My first paying job was in New York. Albert Hammond Jr. from the Strokes paid me and my sister to decorate his best friend's apartment. It was his Christmas present. I painted it the most gorgeous dusty blue, all by myself. I got everything from Kmart and little thrift stores. I tacked up his favorite records—arranged by

color—on the wall. The apartment had a hideous linoleum kitchen floor but we fixed it with a checkerboard of black-and-white peel-and-stick tiles from Home Depot. And we were coming back from buying some stuff and we passed a garden store and found extendable lattice and I said, "Let's buy this and we'll put it behind the couch and hang art!"

E: Some things never change.

L: Everyone who saw it was like "Omigod." It was so good. But for the longest time I was scared to pursue design as a career.

E: I remember when I saw your apartment on Twenty-Second Street in New York and I was like, "Oh my God." I loved it. It was adult, and thought through. I remember that apartment more than any other. You were so confident about it. And I guess I was excited to be there—when I first heard about you, I thought, "Ooh, the Pierces are the coolest girls in all of New York. They only hang out with each other and they're so cool and everybody wants to be them."

L: That's really funny! That apartment felt really good. It felt done. And that was where my late mother-in-law, Carmie, came into play, big-time.

E: And influenced you.

L: Hugely, massively. When we started decorating, I was thinking of going with white walls, but Carmie didn't let me go white. And I wanted to get a TV cabinet from a big retail store that was ivory, creamy, but Carmie was appalled by it! "You cannot buy this cheap crap! If a piece of furniture dings this you will see the wood underneath it. Terrible!" We ended up going to this wonderful vintage store full of Chinese cabinets. Then we played off that. It was a whole new perspective. She bought a suede ottoman that I thought was hideous so I painted over it, periwinkle. With a can of wall paint! We made that place so cozy, and my husband is the greatest chef, so it was like the hangout for all our friends.

E: What did you think of our place on Twelfth Street?

L: I was really impressed when I saw it. That apartment always reminded me of Jimmy Stewart's apartment in *Rear Window*. Very classic romantic New York. When I walked in I thought, "Wow. She knows what she's doing."

E: I didn't really know what I was doing. Well, I knew, but my aunt helped. She's good.

E: Do you remember the night we met?

L: Yes. You said, "My hair's a mess! My hair's a mess! Will you help me fix my hair?" So I remember fixing your hair, doing your make-up. Then I remember putting your number in my phone and for some reason I wrote "Emily ILY." I don't know why. I must have typed your name twice then erased part of it. Anyway, I haven't changed it.

E: That extra ILY is for I Love You.

L: I always knew that I'd be a designer. I know it sounds crazy, but I'm not kidding.

E: You manifested it. Then you forced me into it. Thank the Lord.

CHAPTER THREE

KEEP IT CLASSY

hen in doubt, go classic.

This is a motto for Pierce & Ward. While they love the eccentric and are determinedly eclectic, they are passionate about their classics.

"We avoid trends at all costs and try to find pieces that would've looked great fifty years ago and that will still look great fifty years from now," says Emily.

"Something can be stylish but not be a fad. That's the ideal. Rooms that stand the test of time."

They always include a stately stripe and a French floral for good measure. They love turn-of-the-century sweeping drapes but then cut the drama with a practical mid-century writing desk. They pile kitchen shelves with ethereally delicate teapots then bring them right back down to earth with a solid, scarred butcher block island. They search for quintessential pieces that will be passed down through generations and cherished. There is a depth to some pieces that fads generally lack. Craftsmanship is

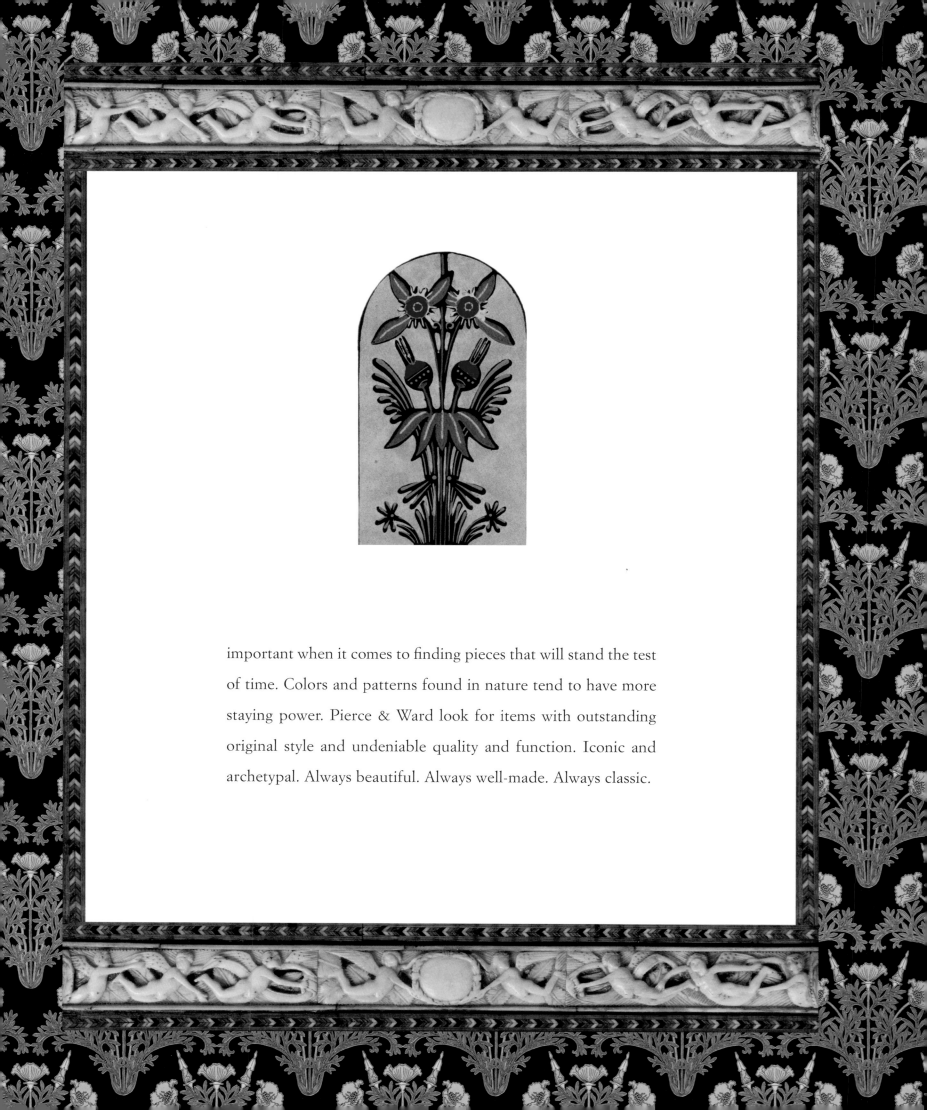

important when it comes to finding pieces that will stand the test of time. Colors and patterns found in nature tend to have more staying power. Pierce & Ward look for items with outstanding original style and undeniable quality and function. Iconic and archetypal. Always beautiful. Always well-made. Always classic.

BRASS TACKS

◆   We love classic, lush florals but always want to cut them with something a bit masculine like a clean, bold stripe so things don't get too sweet.

◆   Remember, creating a room isn't just about visuals. Textures also play a big role in the overall feel. It's about evoking the senses in every way possible.

◆   A lasting look is important to us and we never want rooms to look dated. You can avoid this by keeping the more staple pieces timeless and adding current dashes, like vibrant throw pillows or some metal-framed, modern prints. These things can easily be swapped out if they eventually become tired or trendy.

◆   Antique Persian and Turkish rugs are our favorites. They never go out of style and look fantastic when decked out with contemporary pieces.

◆   Sturdy, handcrafted, natural wood furniture gives weight and maturity to a room. But too much wood of this kind can veer into a lodge vibe so be sure to blend it with upholstery, metals, and even painted wood.

◆   We like to have two, maybe three main colors running the show in a whole house and then an expanded palette for detail. We always ask, what is our focal palette? It's a great starting point.

◆   To create a nice contrast that gives a classic feel, try using a sophisticated shade of paint on the walls and then add playful pops of color with accessories to keep things youthful and fresh.

COZY ELEGANCE

Melanie Griffith's home is a warm Spanish hideaway with incredible bones. She felt it was lacking flow and she needed guidance on how to make certain pieces live comfortably there. Some of her furniture was edging outside of P&W's traditional wheelhouse but instead of pushing against that, we used it as an opportunity to stretch our imagination and it ended up working beautifully. There were some dramatic pieces that just needed a modern spin. She had gorgeous antique lace curtains from Spain and we turned them into Roman shades for the bathroom. The new shape and structure made them feel fresh without losing their vintage charm. A black, gothic wrought-iron banister was dipped in unlacquered brass for some subtle glamour. The house has incredible natural light and we played that up by keeping the wall palette soft with creamy ivories, milky greens, and French grays. The main bathroom underwent the biggest transformation. We gutted it and added a big closet and clawfoot tub under a bay window. The space became super romantic and calming. Melanie is incredibly feminine and elegant so we reflected this by adding lavish touches and covering the house with candles and flowers. Our goal was to create a haven for her.

MELANIE GRIFFITH

My new home is enchanting! I loved working and dreaming and creating with Emily and Louisa. They are full of beautiful, wonderful ideas, and they have such an elegant eye and true style.

CHAPTER FOUR

ECLECTIC AVENUE

hen inspiration comes from every corner of the earth it's nearly impossible to settle on one defined look.

Can a traditional English sofa sit with two wildly retro, 1970s armchairs? Can a boxy, modern coffee table be piled with ancient books and whimsical baubles? Can a pyramid-shaped, peach-velvet headboard be framed with demure floral wallpaper and flanked with Asian lamps? Pierce & Ward proclaim: YES!

Pierce & Ward homes possess qualities that one might look for in a lover . . . beauty, character, strength, sensuality, and a dash of humor. Layered and complex, their rooms keep the interest . . . they romance everyone in them into lingering just a bit longer.

"Even though we draw from so many eras and cultures, we try to find the connection for each piece so it makes sense. There is a method to the madness. We find patterns that work together by collecting samples and layering them. We blend until we have

the right amount of luxury and simplicity," says Emily. "This can mean bringing in a rustic element when there are a lot of refined pieces. We make sure there are hard lines and soft inviting moments."

Louisa continues, "The art of more is not about having a lot of stuff. It's about making your home an unrestricted expression of creativity. We are both untrained designers. We just follow our instincts and go with what moves us. I'm sure we are breaking a million design rules but we don't care as long as it makes us and the clients happy."

THE NEXT LIFE'S
ON ME...

HOLLYWOOD LIFE

FELLINI

ANDY WARHOL
Polaroids 1958–1987

PENGUIN
BOOKS

LOVE
AND OTHER CRIMES

EXPECT THE UNEXPECTED

◆ Eclectic decorating is freeing in the sense that you can pull from any genre that excites you. You can use color, texture, pattern to create a through line that looks complementary rather than cluttered.

◆ Balance hard lines with soft curves, cold metals with warm velvets, reserved English upholsteries with exotic carpets. Eclecticism is about finding a way to marry energies that aren't an obvious match. This style can bring impact in a unique and creative way that's incredibly satisfying to the eye.

◆ Unexpected twists in a home keep things exciting. We love surprising our clients with pieces that might be a nudge outside their comfort zones. Often the objects that at first feel a bit intimidating style-wise end up being their favorites in the end.

Monet

MONET

PAINTING IN NAPLES 1606-1705
FROM CARAVAGGIO TO GIORDANO

DEGAS   Götz Adri

ADEMY OF ARTS

WEIDENFELD
& NICOLSON

Abbeville

New World Visions of
Household Gods & Sacred Places   *Vincent Scully*

ANTOINE WATTEAU   *Donald Posner*

A MAN'S MAN

Josh Brolin's appreciation for detail was an unexpected surprise. We have a passion for what we call "ugly colors" and the fact that he understood the subtleties of using a less-than-pretty color as a backdrop to create a mood or evoke an era thrilled our souls. He let us get our hands on his already wonderful home and give it a bit more direction and soften the edges.

JOSH BROLIN

For someone who's had machismo etched into his face from day one, you would not think interior design would be an obsession of mine. I've never been a messy guy, as I've always loved the personal touch on a home. To me it says everything about a person: what they surround themselves with is, ultimately, what they want to be intrinsically. It's their emotional canvas.

When you see a foyer's background of Italian church steeple stripes mixed with flea market figure paintings you want to write a book. When you see the clean powder Irish green paint on a rustic bookshelf you want to read Joyce by a stone fireplace with a Jameson while you taste the remnants of burned marshmallows still on your lips. Pierce & Ward ignite the imagination and make their homes feel as if there was already a history inside of an era of greatness and debauchery.

CHAPTER FIVE

ORGANIZED ABUNDANCE

ow does one display a lot of special items without overwhelming the eye?

"It's all about making beloved pieces look like a family . . . like they belong together. If you group pieces together on a shelf that have similar tones or perhaps they all have gold or ivory accents . . . you suddenly have a collection rather than a pile of random things," says Louisa.

Emily adds, "Each shelf or display can become its own little world and tell a story about who you are. Include family keepsakes in your designs . . . It's sweet to surround yourself with memories and it gives guests a glimpse into your heritage."

Emily and Louisa recommend filling a home with collections, both inherited and newly acquired. "When you find pieces you love, whether it's pottery or figurines, or works from a particular artist, it's nice to build a collection over time and then you have something to pass on," says Emily. Louisa continues, "I cherish pieces from my late mother-in-law, Carmella Scaggs. Her San Francisco home was filled with incredible treasures

from all over the world that she collected over her lifetime. She personified abundance yet everything was perfectly organized. Her home was magnificent and told the story of her fantastic life so beautifully. After she passed away we kept some of her special pieces that remind us of her. She lives on a bit through them."

To display their treasures, Pierce & Ward have a penchant for tall built-ins framing doorways filled with rows and rows of gold-embossed books, painted teapots, and pottery, punctuated with faces of loved ones in nostalgic black-and-white prints. Their coffee tables run deep and wide to display glass paperweights with suspended artifacts, brass pots filled with flowers or sweets, photography and art books to flip through over a hot cup of tea. Every element invites you to stay, to discover, and to get to know the person living there.

GUSTAVE MOREAU

es McNeill Whistler

ALBRIGHT DÜRER

ALBRECHT DÜRER

Gustave Moreau

GUSTAVE MOREAU

PHOTOGRAPHING MONTANA   DONNA M. LUCEY

W. HOFMANN   GUSTAV KLIMT   NEW YORK GRAPHIC SOCIETY

GUSTAV KLIMT   Women

Angelica Bäumer

SOUTHERN ANTIQUES & FOLK ART

AFRICA   HERB RITTS

Ingres

Jean-Léon Gérôme

TURZER

CY TWOMBLY

CONSCIOUS COLLECTIVE

◆   Vintage toys made of wood and other organic materials can instantly warm a child's space and be a sweet nod to ancestors. They are a welcome change from the disposable plastic toys of today and bring a lovely, earthy energy.

◆   Painting the insides of bookshelves a contrasting color can have a nice impact and make your displays pop. This is an opportunity to go a bit brighter or deeper than you would on a full wall.

◆   Collections and heirlooms are important to us. They can reveal so much personality and character. They carry an energy that conjures memories and stories. Collections can be built over time and passed on for future generations to cherish.

◆   Trays and baskets can give order to otherwise random bits and bobs. We love knick-knacks but we hate clutter! Pick up a few brass or wooden trays from secondhand stores and watch as a messy coffee table suddenly makes sense. Baskets and lovely little decorative boxes can store loose items all over the house and give a cleaner, more together feel.

◆   We are all about collections and abundance—but it's also important to know when to let things go. Check in with yourself a couple of times a year and make sure your space doesn't feel overwhelming and that you aren't verging on clutter. Give items away to friends and family members who might make better use of them or donate to your local thrift shops and charities.

110

KATE THE GREAT

We loved working with Kate Hudson. She has very clear vision and understands that every detail matters. In another life, Kate would be a great home designer! Her eye is super discerning and her taste is adventurous. She gave us license to choose interesting colors and patterns and that always makes our job more fun.

KATE HUDSON

Pierce & Ward make spaces that feel cozy. They pay a lot of attention to detail and really know how to play with color and make bold decisions. I loved their use of stripes and pattern. The colors that we chose were a perfect balance of what I wanted: to be warm but not dark. They were able to keep my home feeling light and airy while maintaining beautiful color and texture.

The "hers" master bathroom was a complete redo and we created a beautiful space. One of my fun bucket list items would be to have a popular Pinterest room! I remember saying to the girls, if we ever took a picture of this bathroom I feel like it would be a very popular pin! The bar-room is my favorite room with a lot of color. We really went there with statement wallpaper and curtains and it's a beautiful mix of colors, green and pink.

One of the things I love about designing homes is pushing the envelope and making decisions that sometimes feel a little scary because they are bold decisions. When they are executed correctly you can create rooms that are truly timeless and something special.

UNDER THE INFLUENCE

LOUISA PIERCE

My late mother-in-law, Carmella "Carmie" Scaggs, was an over-the-top personality with a passion for over-the-top design. We shared a love of mixing low and high style and for finding diamonds in the rough. She inspired me to push boundaries and to be really fearless when making design choices.

EMILY WARD

We affectionately called Carmella a "high-class hoarder" due to her love of collections and stockpiles of fabric and tchotchkes. She definitely influenced the Pierce & Ward philosophy of "more is more."

GOD IS IN THE DETAILS

hy do certain things catch the eye like a silver hook glinting in a murky sea? Why do certain pieces pop and glow as if the spotlight has settled on its muse?

A sculpture as craggy as coral, gray curtains hung like summer storm clouds, weathered wood tables like fallen backyard trees, kitten-soft cashmere blankets. A gentle curve, the right feel and weight, just enough contrast to hold interest, and suddenly an ordinary object becomes a treasure.

Unique gems and one-of-a-kind oddities add personality and depth to every space. Attention paid to small things can have big rewards. As they say, "God is in the details."

"The details can change everything," says Louisa. "An armchair can have a different look depending on whether it's covered in linen, leather, or velvet. Brass fixtures also have a totally different vibe from silver. A room could feel somewhat modern but adding fringed lampshades and Persian rugs could give it a romantic slant. It's all

about adding and taking away until you find the right balance."

Details make a home more personal. When Pierce & Ward shopped for Karen Elson's Nashville home they chose details that reflected the supermodel's trademark looks. "She has beautiful milky skin and a long, graceful neck, so we hunted down brass swan-shaped faucets," says Emily.

"Karen looks like she stepped out of a Klimt painting," continues Louisa. "We chose rich jewel tones and intricate tiles but still kept some modern flair."

"Magical, somewhat whimsical pieces really made sense for her otherworldly essence," says Emily. "Choose details that help your personality shine through."

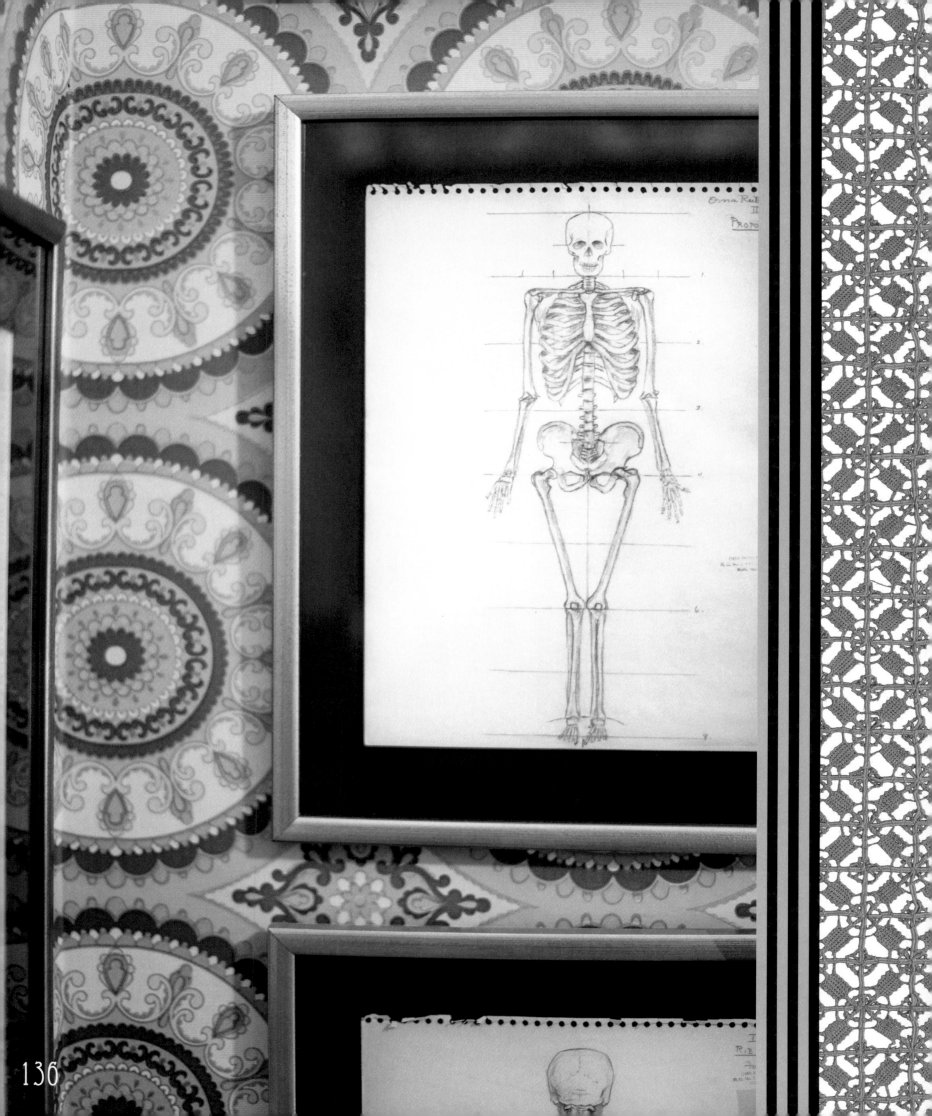

IT'S THE LITTLE THINGS

◆ We love quirky little details inside the home. Animal heads for door knockers and drawer pulls are a trademark of ours. They add whimsy and drama. Faces carved into lamps, animal statues supporting tabletops, swan necks for faucets. . . . There are little characters in all of our homes to keep the people who live there company.

◆ To give a home a sense of balance, add touches of sophistication, sensuality, and humor. Pair a dramatic or risqué photograph with something a bit odd and off-kilter. It's nice to have an obviously beautiful display with a few pieces that are unusual. Push some boundaries to keep things interesting.

◆ We are brass addicts and find that it instantly adds classic glamour to any space. Pops of brass against grayed-down pastels and graphic ivories and blacks is a stunning look that we go back to again and again.

◆ Consider getting crafty with the details. You can find us gluing fringe to lamps, painting coffee tables, re-covering chair cushions . . . All these little touches can add a lot of magic.

◆ Look on eBay for vintage hardware. You will discover gorgeous old pieces that can bring spark back to what you already have. Sometimes you don't need new cabinets . . . you just need new knobs!

WELCOME TO THE DOLLHOUSE

When we first met Emma Roberts, she wanted things minimal and neutral, but through the process she expanded her taste so much and opened up to color and pattern. She's an art lover and a doll collector and we wanted to display her wonderful things in a sophisticated way. We covered her walls with gold-framed paintings and added new pieces to her doll collection. She's also a dedicated reader so we made a space for her to enjoy her books. It's a charming and luxurious home that's just right for her.

EMMA ROBERTS

I bought my house with Emily and Louisa in mind to redo it completely. They transformed the space, not only making it so cozy, eclectic, and feminine, but also changing the entire vibe to suit me. They really listen to what's important to you and put your personality into their design. Everyone who comes to my house says it's so "me." I have a doll collection and Louisa found me the most insane vintage dolls to put on my bookshelf. And because I am obsessed with taking baths, they made my bathroom into a complete oasis with a clawfoot black tub tucked into a gorgeous archway. As if that wasn't enough, they added vintage gold candleholders on the wall. Nothing makes me happier than this part of my house! I also love to read and now I have the coziest reading nook in one of my rooms, with custom cushions as well as a floor-to-ceiling library wall for all my books.

149

WE ARE FAMILY

Our goal was to make Brian Carmody and Christine Jackson's home beautiful but, above all else, it needed to be comfortable. Their family was growing so we made sure the spaces were inviting, solid, and functional without sacrificing character. When you take your immediate needs into consideration and try to create a home that also feels like it's been yours forever, the results can be elegant and efficient . . . and magical.

BRIAN CARMODY

We wanted our house to feel like a lived-in home, not too precious—we were about to have a baby and already had a dog—but with a classiness to the quality of nuance and narrative. Whether it was a lamp or wallpaper, it begged to have a personality and a touch of gravitas or history that came with it. Because of this I feel more at home in our house than in any other house I have ever lived in. I can't pay Pierce & Ward a higher compliment than that.

CHIC WITH A DASH OF SHABBY

 ierce & Ward consider themselves treasure hunters, and the hunt is probably their favorite part of their craft.

When sifting through the ordinary to find the extraordinary, Louisa says she sometimes prefers thrift stores and bargain stores to high-end boutiques. "It's so clear to me when I discover something special in a mountain of junk. It's a thrill to happen upon a totally unique and beautiful item in an unexpected place. We aren't above shopping at discount stores, either! I've scored some incredible finds at T.J. Maxx, believe it or not." Bargain-basement trinkets reside proudly among bespoke pieces in Pierce & Ward homes.

"We have very little snobbery when it comes to where something was found. If we love it, we love it," says Emily.

"But we are particular about whether or not it looks and feels like quality," insists Louisa. "If it feels cheap, it's gotta go."

Every new city they visit provides fresh grounds for the hunt.

They love delicate, unlacquered French tables with legs that curve like a poised deer then drop into intricately carved feet. They swoon over hand-painted Asian screens, alive with flowered paths and birds mid-flight. They always, always buy brass bookends of lions' heads, mouths in a permanent roar, and they can't turn down regal, carved horses in agate and ivory . . . Can one ever have enough? Trays and boxes inlaid with mother-of-pearl and glinting opal keep one's keepsakes organized and accessible.

Are these pieces priceless or were they picked up at a yard sale? If you train your eye to find well-made items with interesting design, no one will know the difference.

ONE MAN'S TRASH

◆ When thrifting for treasures, keep an eye out for things made of earthy materials: woven wooden baskets, homemade clay pottery, brass candlesticks, and carved ivory figurines all can be scored on the right day.

◆ Estate sales are wonderful places to find odds and ends at a bargain. Well-loved pieces with interesting histories add so much to a home.

◆ Sometimes a great item just needs a little love to be restored to its former glory. Look for sturdy craftsmanship, drawers that slide easily, chairs and tables whose joints hold strong even when you give them a wiggle. Seek out interesting lines and small details that make things special.

◆ We love painting old dressers and side tables a creamy olive or a warm coral or gold to turn them into statement pieces.

◆ A beautiful, well-made shade can make a ten-dollar brass lamp look high class.

174

175

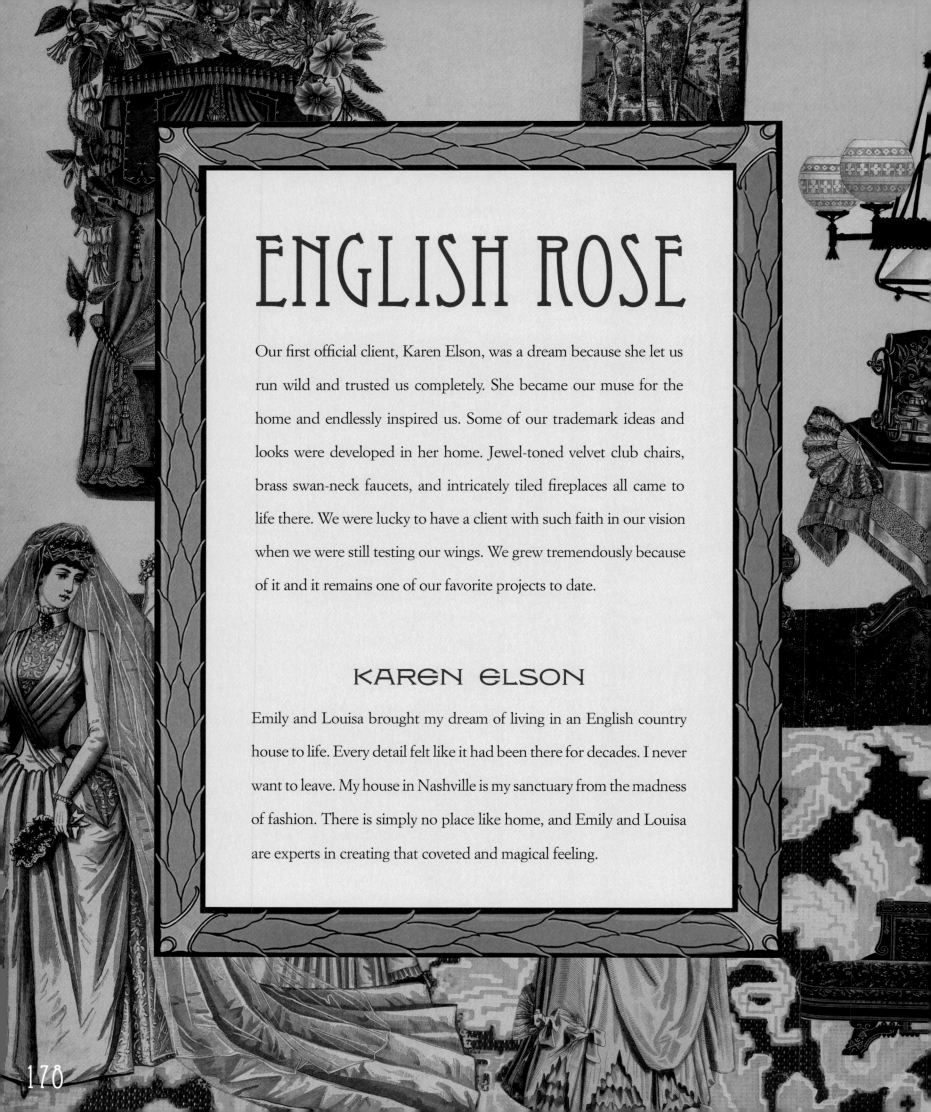

ENGLISH ROSE

Our first official client, Karen Elson, was a dream because she let us run wild and trusted us completely. She became our muse for the home and endlessly inspired us. Some of our trademark ideas and looks were developed in her home. Jewel-toned velvet club chairs, brass swan-neck faucets, and intricately tiled fireplaces all came to life there. We were lucky to have a client with such faith in our vision when we were still testing our wings. We grew tremendously because of it and it remains one of our favorite projects to date.

KAREN ELSON

Emily and Louisa brought my dream of living in an English country house to life. Every detail felt like it had been there for decades. I never want to leave. My house in Nashville is my sanctuary from the madness of fashion. There is simply no place like home, and Emily and Louisa are experts in creating that coveted and magical feeling.

MAGIC HOUR

here are moments as the sun rises and when it sets where a pinky-gold hue cascades over the earth and gently blushes everything in its path. Photographers rise early to capture it and chase it again in the evening until the sun slips behind the horizon. It's called the magic hour . . . and for good reason. It blurs imperfections and infuses an incandescent glow on its subjects. One is suddenly seen in her best light, no rose-colored glasses required. How can we bring this elusive, sought-after light into the home?

"Lamps," says Louisa. "Lots and lots of lamps." Every available surface in Pierce & Ward homes makes space for softly glowing lamps with low-wattage, warm-tinged Edison bulbs.

"Natural lighting is incredibly important and we always keep that in mind when we design, but lighting placement can make or break a space. Nothing kills a vibe more than a stark overhead light. There should be subtle points of light all over the room.

It's so much more inviting and flattering," says Emily.

Louisa muses, "You know that feeling on Christmas morning when you were a kid and you woke up super early as the sun was coming up and the Christmas lights were on the tree and everything just looked like pure magic? That's how we want our rooms to feel."

This is achieved with glittering chandeliers that unabashedly become the main attraction, beveled-glass pendant lights with prism edges, milk-glass globes that hang in trios down hallways like glowing moons to guide one's path . . . and—of course—lamps. Lots and lots of lamps. Let there be light!

STAY GOLD

◆ Create special moments in spaces that could otherwise be overlooked. A sidebar flanked with twin lamps can suddenly have the vibe of an altar. Your favorite piece of art can take center stage and truly get the appreciation it deserves.

◆ Install dimmers wherever possible. Mood adjustment at your fingertips!

◆ You can never have too many lamps. If a corner of a room feels dead and uninviting, it probably needs a beautiful light to draw you in.

◆ Keep the bulb wattage low and warm for that golden-hour sunset glow.

◆ Himalayan salt lamps are affordable and beautiful and give off a flattering, earthy, peachy hue. Look for ones carved into globes or pyramids for a more refined effect.

GILDING THE LILY

We have done two homes for Lily Aldridge and her family and it has been amazing to see her personal style develop over the years. Initially when we'd ask for feedback on decisions, she would declare, "Oh, I don't know! Whatever you guys think!" Now she has a strong sense of what she loves. A bonus to our job is that we get to help our clients sharpen their eye for personal style and become clear about what moves them. Lily's home reflects her beauty, strength, and sweetness and we were honored to be a part of the journey.

LILY ALDRIDGE

I'm so lucky that two of my best friends are also the world's best interior designers! They transform homes into eclectic, unique, beautiful, and cozy spaces you never want to leave.

THERE WILL BE BLOOD

he idea of buying the wrong rug leaves some people frozen in their tracks. The thought of painting a room a shade too dark keeps some people up at night. Designing a home inevitably means making mistakes.

Albert Einstein once said, "A person who never made a mistake, never tried anything new." Sophia Loren echoed this sentiment: "Mistakes are part of the dues one pays for a full life." They understood that with no risk there was no reward. They knew that a life well lived required them to go boldly forward anticipating blunders.

"If you want results that are special, you can't always make safe choices," says Emily. "You happen upon real magic if you're willing to go into risky territory. It doesn't always work but you have to be OK with that."

"Home design is an ongoing process that comes in waves. People change over time and so should the rooms in a home. Keeping in mind that nothing is permanent and

everything can be fixed or redone or repainted takes away some of the terror. It's not always easy having to redo or fix things but it's worth it when you land on something that feels great," says Louisa.

Nail holes can be patched, rooms can be repainted, rugs can be returned, sold, or repurposed. Wallpaper can be torn down, tiles can be ripped out and replaced. A gorgeous, well-loved home is an evolving creation, a livable masterpiece.

KENDALL CHARCOAL
VELVET WHITE

DINING ROOM HALF WALLS

STAIRWELL + DINING HALF WALLS

PONDER ROOM

LIVING ROOM

AR WINDOW COVERINGS

NG ROOM CURTAINS TRIM

LIVING ROOM SOFA OPTION

214

SET THE MOOD

◆ When crafting a mood board, start with broad strokes such as paint colors and wallpaper and then layer in fabrics and key ideas for furniture. Finally, sprinkle your board with details like lamps, knickknacks, and hardware choices. This will give you a reference for the overall vibe and you can return to it if you get off track.

◆ This is a great opportunity to play and experiment before you make any real commitments—so let yourself go a little wild. You may land on something special.

◆ Put your looks together on the board then set everything aside for a while. It's amazing what fresh eyes will do for any project.

◆ Remember: the mood board is meant to serve as a guide and a source of inspiration but always feel free to stray from the plan and regroup if something isn't working in the room.

LET IT SHINE

Carlye Wisel is such a unique individual and we loved the idea of letting her wonderful, quirky spirit shine in the home. Instead of tucking her collections away we decided to make them the stars of the show by creating a place where they could be displayed with real purpose and admired by friends and family.

CARLYE WISEL

Our home turned out to be beyond our wildest dreams, filled with colorful mural-like wallpaper, an inventive built-in that puts all our favorite objects on display, and a fireplace stockpiled with antique treasures. Minimalism is having a moment, and I feared that many of my beloved tchotchkes and objects in my office would need to be removed when the time came—yet quite the opposite happened. Louisa and Emily created an incredible mint green built-in curio cabinet reminiscent of vintage candy shops. They achieved that perfect balance between understanding the way their clients live and injecting the right amount of old-world glamour.

MAXIMALIST

Zoe Schaeffer and her family were really down for anything. Nothing was too out-there for them and that usually results in our most creative spaces. We designed a home where their kids could play and be comfortable, but also a place that kept an air of edge and glamour.

ZOE SCHAEFFER

Our home turned out supremely unique—layered, cozy, warm, harmonious, but also always a bit unexpected. Or, in other terms, "rock star family meets coolest grandma on earth."

The kitchen is our favorite space. We massively reconstructed it and now we do everything there: play board games with the kids, do homework, have family meals, throw back cocktails with friends . . . Plus its perfect cream shade and heavily veined marble and brass tones are striking next to the floral banquette, antique wood tables, and velvet couch. I fought Louisa on the "wagon wheel" light fixture but now I can't imagine this room without it! It just works. I also love the oversize wooden tile flooring in the entry hall, juxtaposed with whimsical pink scenic wallpaper. Maximalist perfection!

THE PIERCE & WARD FAMILY

We would like to thank the Pierce & Ward family,
and all of our loved ones. Without your unwavering support and love,
we would not be where we are today.

AUSTIN SCAGGS

You've been with us since day one. Your steadfast belief in us helped
us to believe in ourselves. Love you forever.

CAITLIN McCALLUM

You set the tone for this book and your creativity always pushes
the boundaries. We are so grateful for your determination and persistence.
Our team would not be complete without you.

CATHERINE PIERCE

Thank you for being able to climb inside our brains and put our design
process into words. Little did we know that when you wrote our bio six years ago
that it would be the inspiration for this book. We love you so much.

ALEX LEVY

Thank you for keeping us in line. We love you endlessly.

YO CUOMO

Thank god we found you because we couldn't have done this any other way.

BOBBIE RICHARDSON

You are a patient wizard—thank you.

CHARLES MIERS & ALIZA FOGELSON

and everyone at Rizzoli, thank you for giving us this opportunity
and helping us bring our work to life in this way.

CREDITS

PAGE 1
Left: Frieze (France), 1815–1825.
Photograph credit: Cooper Hewitt, Smithsonian
Design Museum / Art Resource, NY
Right: © Bradbury & Bradbury Art Wallpapers, Inc.

PAGES 2–3
Left photograph: Leslee Mitchell. Architectural
Digest © Condé Nast
Center: Tiles by William De Morgan, 1839–1917
(manufacturer), and Wedgwood
Right: © State of New South Wales through the State
Archives and Records Authority of NSW 2016
Right center: Shaw, George. *Zoological Lectures
Delivered at the Royal Institution*, ca. 1809
[https://archive.org/details/
zoologicallectur11809shaw/page/n13/mode/2up]

PAGES 4–5
Border: Tiles by William De Morgan, 1839–1917
(manufacturer), and Wedgwood
Right: Seder, Anton. *Die Pflanze in Kunst und
Gewerbe*, ca. 1886 [https://archive.org/details/
diepflanzeinkuns02sede/mode/2up]

PAGES 6–7
Left photograph: Jonny Marlow
Right: Verneuil, M. P. (Maurice Pillard), 1869–1942.
Étude de la Plante, ca. 1903 [https://archive.org/
details/gri_33125005959479/mode/2up]

PAGES 8–9
Top: Border, 1860–1890. Photograph credit:
Cooper Hewitt, Smithsonian Design Museum /
Art Resource, NY
Bottom and sides: © Bradbury & Bradbury Art
Wallpapers, Inc.
Left center: Frieze (France), 1810–1820.
Photograph credit: Cooper Hewitt, Smithsonian
Design Museum / Art Resource, NY

PAGES 10–11
Left and right outer borders: Photograph by
Francis Amiand © *The French Ribbon* /
Pointed Leaf Press / 2014
Left inner border: Game board, 15th century.
Image copyright © The Metropolitan Museum of Art.
Image source: Art Resource, NY
Left photograph: Jonny Marlow
Center: Verneuil, M. P. (Maurice Pillard), 1869–1942.
Étude de la Plante, ca. 1903 [https://archive.org/
details/gri_33125005959479/mode/2up]
Right center: Falck, Jeremias, and Bierpfaff,
Johann Christian. *An Alphabet of Organic Type*.
Rijksmuseum, ca. 1650. Originally published in the
Public Domain Review [https://publicdomainreview.
org/collection/an-alphabet-of-organic-type-ca-1650]

Right bottom: Verneuil, M. P. (Maurice Pillard),
1869–1942. *Étude de la Plante*, ca. 1903 [https://
archive.org/details/gri_33125005959479/mode/2up]

PAGES 12–13
Top: Border, 1860–1890. Photograph credit: Cooper
Hewitt, Smithsonian Design Museum / Art Resource, NY
Left outer border: Photograph by Francis Amiand
© *The French Ribbon* / Pointed Leaf Press / 2014
Bottom left: Verneuil, M. P. (Maurice Pillard), 1869–
1942. *Étude de la Plante*, ca. 1903 [https://archive.
org/details/gri_33125005959479/mode/2up]
Right photograph: Matthew Read

PAGES 14–15
Courtesy of Robert Allen
[https://www.robertallendesign.com]

PAGES 16–17
Left border: Courtesy of Country Floors
[www.countryfloors.com]
Left photograph: Lindsey Rome
Right border: Ribbon (France), ca. 1805.
Photograph credit: Cooper Hewitt, Smithsonian
Design Museum / Art Resource, NY
Right center: Falck, Jeremias, and Bierpfaff,
Johann Christian. *An Alphabet of Organic Type*.
Rijksmuseum, ca. 1650. Originally published in the
Public Domain Review [https://publicdomainreview.
org/collection/an-alphabet-of-organic-type-ca-1650]

PAGES 18–19
Left outer border: Ribbon (France), ca. 1805.
Photograph credit: Cooper Hewitt,
Smithsonian Design Museum / Art Resource, NY
Left inner border: Photograph by Francis Amiand
© *The French Ribbon* / Pointed Leaf Press / 2014
Bottom center: © Ludwig Heinrich, Jungnickel
(1881–1965), *Caricature: Cricket in an Armchair*, 1911.
Image © The Metropolitan Museum of Art. Image
Source: Art Resource, NY
Right inner border: © Bolling & Company
[https://bollingco.com]
Right photograph: Jonny Marlow

PAGES 20–21
Left: © Bolling & Company [https://bollingco.com]
Center: Game board, 15th century. Image copyright
© The Metropolitan Museum of Art. Image source:
Art Resource, NY
Right photograph: Jonny Marlow

PAGES 22–23
Photograph: Jonny Marlow

PAGES 24–25
Photographs: Jonny Marlow
Center: © Bradbury & Bradbury Art Wallpapers, Inc.

PAGES 26–27
Left: Fantin-Latour, Henri, 1836–1904. *Studies of
Female Nudes*, ca. 1895 [https://archive.org/details/
clevelandart-1962.399-studies-of-female-nu]
Photograph: Jonny Marlow

PAGES 28–29
Photographs: Jonny Marlow
Center: *Hydrangea* by Lindsay P. Butterfield, ca. 1896.
Courtesy of Trustworth Studios, David E. Berman

PAGES 30–31
Photograph: Jonny Marlow

PAGES 32–33
Border: Photograph by Francis Amiand
© *The French Ribbon* / Pointed Leaf Press / 2014
Background: © Bradbury & Bradbury Art
Wallpapers, Inc.
Bottom left: Mavelot, Charles, d. 1742. *Nouveau
Livre de differens Cartouches, Couronnes, Casques,
Supports et Tenans*, ca. 1685 [https://archive.org/
details/nouveaulivrededi00mave/mode/2up]
Center photograph: Jonny Marlow

PAGES 34–37
Photograph: Jonny Marlow

PAGES 38–39
Left background: *Temptation*, C. F. A. Voysey, ca. 1889.
Courtesy of Trustworth Studios, David E. Berman
Far left photograph (Louisa Pierce): Tec Petaja
Left inner border: Game board, 15th century.
Image copyright © The Metropolitan Museum of Art.
Image source: Art Resource, NY
Center: Frieze (France), 1810–20.
Photograph credit: Cooper Hewitt, Smithsonian
Design Museum / Art Resource, NY
Right photograph: © Edward Badham

PAGES 40–45
Photograph: © Edward Badham

PAGES 46–47
Left and center: Maison Robert, Ducroquet, Victor.
Book of French Textile Samples, ca. 1863. Originally
published in the *Public Domain Review* [https://
archive.org/details/frenchtextiles00unse/mode/2up]
Right photograph: © Edward Badham

PAGES 48–51
Photograph: © Edward Badham

PAGES 52–53
Right background: Verneuil, M. P. (Maurice Pillard),
1869–1942. *Étude de la Plante*, ca. 1903 [https://
archive.org/details/gri_33125005959479/mode/2up]
Right inner border: Anonymous. *Siersloop van linnen
met een voorpand van naaldkant met het wapen van België*,

ca. 1914–ca. 1918 [https://www.rijksmuseum.nl/nl/collectie/bk-1978-42]
Right artwork: Oil painting by Caitlin McCallum

PAGES 54–55
Top: Dresser, Christopher, 1834–1904. Two frieze of dado-rail ornaments. Photograph credit: The New York Public Library / Art Resource, NY
Bottom: © Bradbury & Bradbury Art Wallpapers, Inc.

PAGES 56–57
Background: Verneuil, M. P. (Maurice Pillard), 1869–1942. *Étude de la Plante*, ca. 1903 [https://archive.org/details/gri_33125005959479/mode/2up]
Left inner border: Photographs by Francis Amiand © *The French Ribbon* / Pointed Leaf Press / 2014
Left photograph: Jonny Marlow
Right center: Falck, Jeremias, and Bierpfaff, Johann Christian. *An Alphabet of Organic Type*. Rijksmuseum, ca. 1650. Originally published in the *Public Domain Review* [https://publicdomainreview.org/collection/an-alphabet-of-organic-type-ca-1650]

PAGES 58–59
Left background: Verneuil, M. P. (Maurice Pillard), 1869–1942. *Étude de la Plante*, ca. 1903 [https://archive.org/details/gri_33125005959479/mode/2up]
Left inner border: Game board, 15th century. Image copyright © The Metropolitan Museum of Art. Image source: Art Resource, NY
Left center: Verneuil, M. P. (Maurice Pillard), 1869–1942. *Étude de la Plante*, ca. 1903 [https://archive.org/details/gri_33125005959479/mode/2up]
Right photograph: Caitlin McCallum

PAGES 60–61
Photograph: Caitlin McCallum
Right: Anonymous. *Strook naaldkant met oogjespatroon*, ca. 1790–ca. 1799 [https://www.rijksmuseum.nl/en/search/objects?q=bk-br-j-294&p=1&ps=12&st=objects&ii=0#/bk-br-j-294,0]

PAGES 62–63
Left photograph: Jonny Marlow
Center: © Bradbury & Bradbury Art Wallpapers, Inc.
Right photograph: Caitlin McCallum

PAGES 64–65
Photograph: © Edward Badham

PAGES 66–67
Background photograph: Caitlin McCallum
Right inner border: Game board, 15th century. Image copyright © The Metropolitan Museum of Art. Image source: Art Resource, NY
Right photograph: Rosie D'Argenzio

PAGES 68–73
Photograph: Jonny Marlow

PAGES 74–75
Left photograph: Jonny Marlow
Right: *Cromer Bird*. Furnishing fabric, ca. 1884. Photograph credit: V&A Images, London / Art Resource, NY

PAGES 76–77
Photograph: Jonny Marlow

PAGES 78–79
Mythical Land wallpaper, Kit Kemp for Andrew Martin [www.andrewmartin.co.uk]

PAGES 80–83
Photographs: Jonny Marlow

PAGES 84–85
Left outer border: Anonymous. *Table carpet with the four elements and a strewn floral pattern*, ca. 1650 [https://www.rijksmuseum.nl/nl/collectie/bk-1975-75]
Left inner border: Game board, 15th century. Image copyright © The Metropolitan Museum of Art. Image source: Art Resource, NY
Left photograph: Jonny Marlow
Right border: *Length of Fabric for Clothing*, 18th century. Image copyright © The Metropolitan Museum of Art. Image source: Art Resource, NY
Right center: Falck, Jeremias, and Bierpfaff, Johann Christian. *An Alphabet of Organic Type*. Rijksmuseum, ca. 1650. Originally published in the *Public Domain Review* [https://publicdomainreview.org/collection/an-alphabet-of-organic-type-ca-1650]

PAGES 86–87
Left border: *Length of Fabric for Clothing*, 18th century. Image copyright © The Metropolitan Museum of Art. Image source: Art Resource, NY
Left center: Illustration by Catherine Pierce
Right photograph: © Edward Badham

PAGES 88–89
Photograph: Jonny Marlow

PAGES 90–91
Left photograph: Jonny Marlow
Right background: © Bradbury & Bradbury Art Wallpapers, Inc.
Bottom right: Illustration by Catherine Pierce

PAGES 92–93
Photograph: Jonny Marlow

PAGES 94–95
Photograph: © Edward Badham

PAGES 96–97
Left background: *Mythical Land* wallpaper, Kit Kemp for Andrew Martin [www.andrewmartin.co.uk]
Right photograph: Carmen-Jean Cluttey

PAGES 98–99
Photograph: Jonny Marlow

PAGES 100–101
Left photograph: Leslee Mitchell. Architectural Digest © Condé Nast
Top right: Maison Robert, Ducroquet, Victor. *Book of French Textile Samples*, ca. 1863. Originally published in the *Public Domain Review* [https://archive.org/details/frenchtextiles00unse/mode/2up]
Bottom right: Untitled (Ducks), ca. 1870. Photograph credit: V&A Images, London / Art Resource, NY

PAGES 102–105
Photograph: © Edward Badham

PAGES 106–107
Left outer border: Verneuil, M. P. (Maurice Pillard), 1869–1942. *Étude de la Plante*, ca. 1903 [https://archive.org/details/gri_33125005959479/mode/2up]
Left inner border: Photograph by Francis Amiand © *The French Ribbon* / Pointed Leaf Press / 2014
Left photograph: Jonny Marlow
Right border: Photograph by Francis Amiand © *The French Ribbon* / Pointed Leaf Press / 2014
Right center: Falck, Jeremias, and Bierpfaff, Johann Christian. *An Alphabet of Organic Type*. Rijksmuseum, ca. 1650. Originally published in the *Public Domain Review* [https://publicdomainreview.org/collection/an-alphabet-of-organic-type-ca-1650]

PAGES 108–109
Left outer border: Photograph by Francis Amiand © *The French Ribbon* / Pointed Leaf Press / 2014
Left inner border: Verneuil, M. P. (Maurice Pillard), 1869–1942. *Étude de la Plante*, ca. 1903 [https://archive.org/details/gri_33125005959479/mode/2up]
Right photograph: Jonny Marlow

PAGES 110–113
Photographs: © Edward Badham

PAGES 114–115
Left photograph: Jonny Marlow
Center: *The Demon*, C. F. A. Voysey, ca. 1889. Trustworth Studios, David E. Berman
Right photograph: © Edward Badham

PAGES 116–117
Left photograph: © Edward Badham
Right: Photograph by Francis Amiand © *The French Ribbon* / Pointed Leaf Press / 2014

PAGES 118–119
Photographs: Jonny Marlow
Center: Courtesy of Robert Allen [https://www.robertallendesign.com]

PAGES 120–121
Background: © Bolling & Company [https://bollingco.com]
Left center: Fraktur drawing, unknown maker, Pennsylvania, 1795–1830. Bequest of Henry Francis du Pont, courtesy of Winterthur Museum

PAGES 122–123
Photographs: Jonny Marlow
Center: © Bolling & Company [https://bollingco.com]

PAGES 124–125
Left photograph: Jonny Marlow
Center: Photograph by Francis Amiand © *The French Ribbon* / Pointed Leaf Press / 2014
Right photograph: © Edward Badham

PAGES 126–127
Background: Courtesy of Les Indiennes [https://lesindiennes.com]
Top and bottom border: © Bradbury & Bradbury Art Wallpapers, Inc.
Left inner border: Photograph by Francis Amiand © *The French Ribbon* / Pointed Leaf Press / 2014

PAGES 128–129
Left background and right borders: Verneuil, M. P. (Maurice Pillard), 1869–1942. *Étude de la Plante*, ca. 1903 [https://archive.org/details/gri_33125005959479/mode/2up]
Left photograph: Jonny Marlow
Right center: Falck, Jeremias, and Bierpfaff, Johann Christian. *An Alphabet of Organic Type.* Rijksmuseum, ca. 1650. Originally published in the *Public Domain Review* [https://publicdomainreview.org/collection/an-alphabet-of-organic-type-ca-1650]

PAGES 130–131
Left outer borders: Verneuil, M. P. (Maurice Pillard), 1869–1942. *Étude de la Plante*, ca. 1903 [https://archive.org/details/gri_33125005959479/mode/2up]
Bottom left inner border: Frieze (USA), ca. 1905. Photograph credit: Cooper Hewitt, Smithsonian Design Museum / Art Resource, NY
Right photograph: Caitlin McCallum

PAGES 132–135
Photograph: Caroline Allison

PAGES 136–137
Left photograph: Leslee Mitchell. Architectural Digest © Condé Nast
Center: Anonymous. *Gordijnrand van kloskant met geometrische figuren en franje*, ca. 1800–before 1936 [https://www.rijksmuseum.nl/en/search/objects?q=bk-14868&p=1&ps=12&st=objects&ii=0#/bk-14868,0]
Right photograph: Matthew Read

PAGES 138–139
Left photograph: Caitlin McCallum
Bottom left: Grasset, Eugène. *La Plante et ses Applications Ornementales*, ca. 1896 [https://library.si.edu/digital-library/book/planteetsesappl00gras]
Center: Valence for a bed (*Lit à la duchesse en impériale*), ca. 1780–1790. Image copyright © The Metropolitan Museum of Art. Image source: Art Resource, NY
Right background: Grasset, Eugène. *La Plante et ses Applications Ornementales*, ca. 1896 [https://library.si.edu/digital-library/book/planteetsesappl00gras]

PAGES 140–141
Left photograph: © Edward Badham
Right: Game board, 15th century. Image copyright © The Metropolitan Museum of Art. Image source: Art Resource, NY

PAGES 142–145
Photographs: © Edward Badham

PAGES 146–147
Border: Game board, 15th century. Image copyright © The Metropolitan Museum of Art. Image source: Art Resource, NY
Photograph: © Edward Badham

PAGES 148–149
Left photograph: © Edward Badham
Right photograph: Matthew Read

PAGES 150–151
Photograph: © Edward Badham

Bottom border: Verneuil, M. P. (Maurice Pillard), 1869–1942. *Étude de la Plante*, ca. 1903 [https://archive.org/details/gri_33125005959479/mode/2up]

PAGES 152–153
Photographs: Matthew Read

PAGES 154–155
Photographs: Caitlin McCallum
Center: Maison Robert, Ducroquet, Victor. *Book of French Textile Samples*, ca. 1863. Originally published in the *Public Domain Review* [https://archive.org/details/frenchtextiles00unse/mode/2up]

PAGES 156 –157
Left background: Knox, Archibald, 1864–1933. Photograph credit: V&A Images, London / Art Resource, NY
Right photograph: Caitlin McCallum

PAGES 158–159
Left photograph: Caitlin McCallum
Center: Dresser, Christopher, 1834–1904. Two frieze of dado-rail ornaments. Photograph credit: The New York Public Library / Art Resource, NY
Right photograph: Jonny Marlow

PAGES 160–161
Left inner border: Courtesy of Fabricut [https://www.fabricut.com]
Left photograph: Leslee Mitchell. Architectural Digest © Condé Nast
Right border: © Bradbury & Bradbury Art Wallpapers, Inc.
Right center: Falck, Jeremias, and Bierpfaff, Johann Christian. *An Alphabet of Organic Type.* Rijksmuseum, ca. 1650. Originally published in the *Public Domain Review* [https://publicdomainreview.org/collection/an-alphabet-of-organic-type-ca-1650]

PAGES 162–163
Outer border: © Bradbury & Bradbury Art Wallpapers, Inc.
Top left center: Verneuil, M. P. (Maurice Pillard), 1869–1942. *Étude de la Plante*, ca. 1903 [https://archive.org/details/gri_33125005959479/mode/2up]
Bottom left center: © Bradbury & Bradbury Art Wallpapers, Inc.
Right photograph: Leslee Mitchell. Architectural Digest © Condé Nast

PAGES 164–165
Photographs: Leslee Mitchell. Architectural Digest © Condé Nast
Center: Verneuil, M. P. (Maurice Pillard), 1869–1942. *Étude de la Plante*, ca. 1903 [https://archive.org/details/gri_33125005959479/mode/2up]

PAGES 166–167
Left background: © Bradbury & Bradbury Art Wallpapers, Inc.
Left inner border: Photograph by Francis Amiand © *The French Ribbon* / Pointed Leaf Press / 2014
Right photograph: Leslee Mitchell. Architectural Digest © Condé Nast

PAGES 168–169
Photographs: Leslee Mitchell. Architectural Digest © Condé Nast
Center: Verneuil, M. P. (Maurice Pillard), 1869–1942. *Étude de la Plante*, ca. 1903 [https://archive.org/details/gri_33125005959479/mode/2up]

PAGES 170–171
Photographs: Leslee Mitchell. Architectural Digest © Condé Nast
Center: Frieze (France), 1825–1835. Designed by Xavier Mader. Photograph credit: Cooper Hewitt, Smithsonian Design Museum / Art Resource, NY

PAGES 172–173
Left photograph: Leslee Mitchell. Architectural Digest © Condé Nast
Wallpaper: *Coven* in Mahogany by Maison C. [http://www.maisonc.com]
Right: Anonymous. *Woman's Haori with White and Red Cranes*, ca. 1920–1940 [https://www.rijksmuseum.nl/en/collection/ak-rak-2009-3-37]

PAGES 174–175
Left: *Waverly Olana Bay Leaf.* Courtesy of Iconix Brand Group, Inc.
Center: Cape for an ecclesiastical figurine (France), mid-19th century. Photo credit: Cooper Hewitt, Smithsonian Design Museum / Art Resource, NY
Right: Courtesy of Fabricut [https://www.fabricut.com]
Borders: Verneuil, M. P. (Maurice Pillard), 1869–1942. *Étude de la Plante*, ca. 1903 [https://archive.org/details/gri_33125005959479/mode/2up]

PAGES 176–177
Photographs: Leslee Mitchell. Architectural Digest © Condé Nast
Center: © Bradbury & Bradbury Art Wallpapers, Inc.

PAGES 178–179
Background: Anonymous, 19th century. Untitled (Victorian collage). 1880–1890. Photography credit: Smithsonian American Art Museum, Washington, DC / Art Resource, NY
Left inner border: Seder, Anton. *Die Pflanze in Kunst und Gewerbe*, ca. 1886 [https://archive.org/details/diepflanzeinkuns02sede/mode/2up]
Right inner border: Maison Robert, Ducroquet, Victor. *Book of French Textile Samples*, ca. 1863. Originally published in the *Public Domain Review* [https://archive.org/details/frenchtextiles00unse/mode/2up]
Right photograph: © Edward Badham

PAGES 180–181
Photographs: Leslee Mitchell. Architectural Digest © Condé Nast
Center: Verneuil, M. P. (Maurice Pillard), 1869–1942. *Étude de la Plante*, ca. 1903 [https://archive.org/details/gri_33125005959479/mode/2up]

PAGES 182–183
Left border: © Bradbury & Bradbury Art Wallpapers, Inc.
Left photograph: © Edward Badham
Right center: Falck, Jeremias, and Bierpfaff, Johann Christian. *An Alphabet of Organic Type.* Rijksmuseum,

ca. 1650. Originally published in the *Public Domain Review* [https://publicdomainreview.org/collection/an-alphabet-of-organic-type-ca-1650]

PAGES 184–185
Left center top and bottom: © Bolling & Company [https://bollingco.com]
Center: © Bradbury & Bradbury Art Wallpapers, Inc.
Right photograph: © Edward Badham

PAGES 186–187
Photograph: Jonny Marlow

PAGES 188–189
Left: Maison Robert, Ducroquet, Victor. *Book of French Textile Samples*, ca. 1863. Originally published in the *Public Domain Review* [https://archive.org/details/frenchtextiles00unse/mode/2up]
Bottom left: Shaw, George. *Zoological Lectures Delivered at the Royal Institution*, ca. 1809 [https://archive.org/details/zoologicallectur11809shaw/page/n13/mode/2up]
Right photograph: Caitlin McCallum

PAGES 190–191
Photograph: © Edward Badham

PAGES 192–193
Border: Verneuil, M. P. (Maurice Pillard), 1869–1942. *Étude de la Plante*, ca. 1903 [https://archive.org/details/gri_33125005959479/mode/2up]
Photograph: Jonny Marlow

PAGES 194–195
Photograph: Jonny Marlow

PAGES 196–197
Left photograph: © Edward Badham
Center: Van De Kamer, Johanna. *Romaans bandmotief met vlechtwerk*, ca. 1890–1922 [https://www.rijksmuseum.nl/en/collection/RP-T-1997-58-17(R)]
Right photograph: Jonny Marlow

PAGES 198–199
Photograph: Carmen-Jean Cluttey

PAGES 200–201
Left photograph: Caitlin McCallum
Center: Anonymous. *Siersloop van linnen met een voorpand van naaldkant met het wapen van België*, ca. 1914–1918 [https://www.rijksmuseum.nl/nl/collectie/bk-1978-42]
Right photograph: Jonny Marlow

PAGES 202–203
Photograph: Caitlin McCallum

PAGES 204–205
Photograph: Jonny Marlow
Right: Grasset, Eugène. *La Plante et ses Applications Ornementales*, ca. 1896 [https://library.si.edu/digital-library/book/planteetsesappl00gras]

PAGES 206–207
Left inner border: Anonymous. *"Cave canem" Mosaic in the House of the Tragic Poet*, Pompeii, ca. 1865–1875 [https://www.rijksmuseum.

nl/en/search/objects?q=rp-f-f01087-bg&p=1&ps=12&st=objects&ii=0#/rp-f-f01087-bg,0]
Right border: Game board, 15th century. Image copyright © The Metropolitan Museum of Art. Image source: Art Resource, NY
Right center: Falck, Jeremias, and Bierpfaff, Johann Christian. *An Alphabet of Organic Type*. Rijksmuseum, ca. 1650. Originally published in the *Public Domain Review* [https://publicdomainreview.org/collection/an-alphabet-of-organic-type-ca-1650]

PAGES 208–209
Left border: Game board, 15th century. Image copyright © The Metropolitan Museum of Art. Image source: Art Resource, NY
Left center top and bottom: Seder, Anton. *Die Pflanze in Kunst und Gewerbe*, ca. 1886 [https://archive.org/details/diepflanzeinkuns02sede/mode/2up]
Right photograph: Caitlin McCallum

PAGES 210–211
Right photograph: Leslee Mitchell. Architectural Digest © Condé Nast

PAGES 212–213
Photograph: Caitlin McCallum

PAGES 214–215
Center: Frieze (France), 1815–1825. Photography credit: Cooper Hewitt, Smithsonian Design Museum / Art Resource, NY
Right background: Courtesy of Fabricut [https://www.fabricut.com]
Bottom right center: Shaw, George. *Zoological Lectures Delivered at the Royal Institution*, ca. 1809 [https://archive.org/details/zoologicallectur11809shaw/page/n13/mode/2up]

PAGES 216–217
Photographs: Caitlin McCallum

PAGES 218–219
Left outer border: Anonymous. *Kimono for an unmarried woman*, ca. 1905–1920 [https://www.rijksmuseum.nl/en/search/objects?q=ak-rak-2009-3-1&p=1&ps=12&st=objects&ii=0#/ak-rak-2009-3-1,0]
Left inner border: Verneuil, M. P. (Maurice Pillard), 1869–1942. *Étude de la Plante*, ca. 1903 [https://archive.org/details/gri_33125005959479/mode/2up]
Right inner border: Seder, Anton. *Die Pflanze in Kunst und Gewerbe*, ca. 1886 [https://archive.org/details/diepflanzeinkuns02sede/mode/2up]

PAGES 220–221
Background: Verneuil, M. P. (Maurice Pillard), 1869–1942. *Étude de la Plante*, ca. 1903 [https://archive.org/details/gri_33125005959479/mode/2up]
Top right inner border: Game board, 15th century. Image copyright © The Metropolitan Museum of Art. Image source: Art Resource, NY
Bottom right inner border: Game board, 15th century. Image copyright © The Metropolitan Museum of Art. Image source: Art Resource, NY

PAGES 222–223
Photographs: Caitlin McCallum
Center: *Sevilla Verde Piedra* by the Rosa Bernal Collection at Claremont Furnishing Fabrics

PAGES 224–225
Background: © Bradbury & Bradbury Art Wallpapers, Inc.
Top far left: Tassels. Late 17th to early 18th century. Photograph credit: Cooper Hewitt, Smithsonian Design Museum / Art Resource, NY
Top left inner border: Game board, 15th century. Image copyright © The Metropolitan Museum of Art. Image source: Art Resource, NY
Top left center: Illustration by Caitlin McCallum
Bottom left inner border: Photograph by Francis Amiand © *The French Ribbon* / Pointed Leaf Press / 2014

PAGES 226–227
Photograph: Jonny Marlow

PAGES 228–229
Left photograph: Caitlin McCallum
Right: Fantin-Latour, Henri, 1836–1904. *Studies of Female Nudes*, ca. 1895 [https://archive.org/details/clevelandart-1962.399-studies-of-female-nu]

PAGES 230–231
Photograph: Leslee Mitchell. Architectural Digest © Condé Nast

PAGES 232–233
Right background: *Sevilla Verde Piedra* by the Rosa Bernal Collection at Claremont Furnishing Fabrics
Right inner border: Seder, Anton. *Die Pflanze in Kunst und Gewerbe*, ca. 1886 [https://archive.org/details/diepflanzeinkuns02sede/mode/2up]

PAGE 234
Photograph: Jonny Marlow

PAGE 240
Center: De Kemp, Nicolaes (attributed to). *Title page with cartouche surrounded by four allegorical figures*, ca. 1590–1593 [https://www.rijksmuseum.nl/en/search/objects?set=NG-2011-98#/NG-2011-98-1,1]

We made every effort to trace the ownership of all copyrighted material and to secure the necessary permissions to include the content as you see it in this volume. We extend our apologies for any inaccuracies or inadvertent omissions, and our grateful acknowledgments to the above contributors and sources, which all had a hand in the making of this book.

First published in the United States of America in 2020 by
Rizzoli International Publications, Inc.
300 Park Avenue South
New York, NY 10010
www.rizzoliusa.com

Copyright © 2020 Pierce & Ward LLC
Image credits appear on pages 235–238.

Publisher: Charles Miers
Editor: Aliza Fogelson
Book Design: Yolanda Cuomo Design
Senior Designer: Bobbie Richardson
Research and Creative Curation: Caitlin McCallum
Retoucher: Mark Davis
Production Manager: Kaija Markoe
Managing Editor: Lynn Scrabis

Printed in Italy
2020 2021 2022 2023 / 10 9 8 7 6 5 4 3 2 1
ISBN: 978-0-8478-6383-9
Library of Congress Control Number: 2020935913

Visit us online:
Facebook.com/RizzoliNewYork
Twitter: @Rizzoli_Books
Instagram.com/RizzoliBooks
Pinterest.com/RizzoliBooks
Youtube.com/user/RizzoliNY
issuu.com/Rizzoli